AGAINST ALL ODDS
(Reminisce Life Journey)

Abiodun Adeyemi, PhD

Published by Dolman Scott in 2025

Copyright © 2025 Abiodun Adeyemi

All rights reserved. No part of this publication may be reproduced, stored in a retrieval system, or transmitted in any form or by any means, electronic, mechanical, photocopy, recording or otherwise, without prior written permission of the copyright owner. Nor can it be circulated in any form of binding or cover other than that in which it is published and without similar condition including this condition being imposed on a subsequent purchaser.

ISBN Printed book: 978-1-915351-40-1
ISBN eBook: 978-1-915351-41-8

Published by
DolmanScott
www.dolmanscott.com

Dedication

I want to express my deep appreciation to my mother, whose unwavering love and nurturing support have consistently guided my life. Her remarkable qualities have significantly influenced my personal and professional development.

Furthermore, I acknowledge my wife, who embodies both beauty and strength. Her steadfast dedication and countless sacrifices have established a solid foundation for my journey, enriching our lives together and inspiring me daily.

My children represent the greatest source of joy in my life. Their vibrant energy and inquisitive nature bring vitality and fulfilment, akin to a thriving orchard filled with olive trees, signifying resilience and growth.

I am also grateful for the numerous individuals who have shared my journey. Their contributions and insights have significantly enhanced my understanding and walk with God. May this narrative serve as a source of inspiration and resonate with all who engage with it.

Contents

Foreword vii

Acknowledgements xi

Preface xiii

Introduction xvii

Chapter 1: *Navigating Early Uncertainties* 1

Chapter 2: *Charting A New Course* 11

Chapter 3: *Establishing Strong Foundations* 25

Chapter 4: *Impressions That Endure* 39

Chapter 5: *The Inner Anchors* 57

Chapter 6: *A Transformative Journey* 67

Chapter 7: *The God Factor* 77

Chapter 8: *Rise Above Prejudice/Discrimination* 85

Glossary 95

Foreword

Dr. Abiodun Adeyemi provides a reflective journey through the highs and lows of human experience in the following pages, revealing how even the most severe adversity may serve as a springboard for personal growth. It is a privilege for me to write this foreword for *Against All Odds*, a book that tells a great story and encourages readers to be resilient, hopeful, and strong.

The book's narrative speaks to a universal truth: even though the road may seem lonely and full of challenges, we are destined for our own kind of greatness. From financial difficulties to the lack of a father figure, from his mother's sacrifices to difficulties fulfilling his academic goals, his story is filled with tribulations that would test anyone's fortitude. He nevertheless discovered an "inner anchor" that sustained him through every trial; it was an anchor composed of love, faith, fortitude, and an unbreakable spirit.

Throughout this book, we see the resilience of community and family as hidden heroes—especially three women who greatly impacted his life—emerge as sources of courage, support, and healing. Dr. Adeyemi's experiences show that having a strong support system around oneself during difficult times is beneficial and necessary. On his path to achievement, these individuals served as pillars of support, remedies for hopelessness, and steady allies.

Anyone who has felt their aspirations slip away can relate to Dr. Adeyemi's story of pursuing a PhD despite overwhelming circumstances. He refused to let his studies come to an end when financing was abruptly cut off. As an example of the human spirit's tenacity and the strength of hope, he persisted, finished his doctorate in medical physics, and started a 30-year career with the UK National Health Service.

His story reminds us that our obstacles don't have to define who we are or what we can achieve. He provides deep insights on creating a life of meaning by sharing his thoughts on forgiveness, family love, and the importance of inner resilience—not by ignoring our struggles but by overcoming them.

Against All Odds is more than an autobiography; it serves as a manual for everyone looking for motivation to get through their own struggles. It teaches us that although our circumstances and surroundings may impact us, they do not define our fate. It is up to us to decide who we want to be. Dr. Adeyemi encourages us to embrace resilience, choose hope over despair, and succeed in our own lives by sharing his life story.

Foreword

    This book is a celebration of the human spirit's capacity to overcome adversity, a testimony to our influence on other people's lives, and a call to acknowledge the grace that can guide us toward more promising and hopeful futures. As you read these pages, I hope you will have the fortitude and resolve to take on your own challenges.

    Temitope Ologunoye, PhD
    Co-Founder, RadiantLink Ministries

Acknowledgements

This journey, like many others in life, was not traversed alone. I am grateful for the incredible individuals God placed in my path, each offering invaluable support, wisdom, and unwavering love throughout this expedition.

First and foremost, my beloved wife, Olabimpe. Your steadfast love, immense sacrifices, and endless encouragement have served as my guiding compass. In moments of self-doubt, you remained a beacon of belief in my abilities and aspirations, reminding me of my potential and igniting the flame of hope within me. Thank you for your relentless support, for being my partner in every sense, and for believing in our shared dreams.

To my cherished children, Ayodeji and Bolanle, you are my constant source of joy and inspiration. Your unfiltered admiration and love empower me to be a better version of myself. Knowing that you look up to me fills my heart with purpose and pushes me to strive for excellence for my sake and yours. Thank you for being my shining example of unconditional love.

I owe a debt of gratitude to the countless individuals who have crossed my path and touched my life profoundly, whether through encouragement, mentorship, or simply being present during difficult moments. Each interaction has imparted invaluable lessons that have shaped my character and fortified my resolve.

Above all, I express my deepest gratitude to my Heavenly Father, God, Creator, and Sustainer, the true mentor and an unparalleled friend. Your consistent support, gentle challenges, and steady counsel have greatly aided my life's path. Your love, divine wisdom, and provision have continually served as vital resources. I treasure the serene mornings we share in fellowship, where your word brings illumination to my heart and clarity to my mind. Thank you for your enduring grace, steadfast love, and the incredible privilege of serving you.

Preface

Genesis 1:3 (NIV)

"And God said, let there be light, and there was light."

Preface

This narrative I am about to unfold is not a tale of extraordinary achievements or worldly accolades; rather, it embodies the account of life traversed through myriad uncertainties and personal convictions, all meticulously guided by faith and nurtured by the grace of God.

My journey has been far from smooth sailing, laden with challenges, doubts, and significant moments of introspection. These experiences have contributed to my evolving understanding of personal conviction, resilience, diligence, and the transformative power of perseverance. Through this life lens, I needed to know true growth.

In the subsequent pages, I will share my story against three distinct backdrops: my formative years marked by uncertainties, the professional pathways I ventured through, and the eventual transition into ministry. The objective here is not to boast about personal accomplishments or highlight worldly achievements but to open my heart and share insights that may help dispel the lingering doubts in the lives of others. I hope this narrative resonates with many on their journeys of discovery, seeking direction, or yearning for meaning and the ability to triumph over considerable odds.

My life experiences illustrate that success and greatness are subjective, though entirely attainable. They are subjective in numerous ways, encompassing how individuals measure and value their lives compared to others. The essence of greatness is intricately woven into our human DNA, a divine imprint from God. This concept was beautifully depicted in the Bible in Luke 1:15 and 1:32, where it was proclaimed that John the Baptist and Jesus would be great. These individuals grew not merely due to their birthright or material wealth but through the abundant gifts of grace bestowed upon them and through their commitment to service and purpose. Through God's infallible word, we understand that everyone is destined for their unique form of greatness in Christ.

Reflecting on the wisdom of Zig Ziglar, "You don't have to be great to start, but you have to start to be great," I am reminded that every journey begins with a single step.

As you immerse yourself in this narrative, may it inspire you to pursue the greatness within you. I hope my story serves as a source of inspiration, guiding you toward the same enduring grace that can empower you to face and conquer daunting challenges.

Introduction

Psalm 5:3 (NIV)

"In the morning, Lord, you hear my voice; in the morning I lay my requests before you and wait expectantly."

Introduction

From the thick fog of uncertainty that enveloped my early childhood to the bright clarity of purpose that eventually illuminated my later years, my life journey is a powerful testament to the transformative influence of divine intervention and grace. Many individuals have sought to document the unique events that have shaped their lives, recounting their triumphs against formidable odds. Inspired by such narratives, I feel compelled to share my story, which illustrates how adversity can lead to growth—making us stronger, wiser, and more resilient. We understand ourselves deeper through the accumulation of trials and tribulations, setbacks, and victories.

I was born and raised in a community where everyone knew one another, a nurturing environment that gave rise to support and familiarity. However, my early years were marked by the absence of my biological mother, who was not present until my middle childhood, and my biological father, whose presence only emerged during my adulthood. In this emotionally turbulent landscape, I found solace and unconditional love in the warm embrace of my grandparents. Their steadfast support was essential to my emotional development, teaching me invaluable lessons about love, compassion, and the significance of belonging. These formative experiences instilled in me an early appreciation for the most critical aspects of parenting—understanding, sacrifice, and unconditional love.

As I navigated the complexities of life, I forged a path through the realms of education, career ambitions, and personal challenges. This journey was often fraught with difficulties, including the struggle to secure necessities and a stable family environment. Amid these adversities, I began to sense a deep calling—a whisper of purpose that urged me to transcend the limitations imposed by circumstances. This calling ignited a fire, propelling me toward a life marked by determination and hope, ultimately opening the gates to personal fulfilment.

This story is a chronicled evolution of my journey, tracking my path from initial uncertainty to embracing a life devoted to God. It delves into my trials and triumphs, including the courageous decision to leave behind a successful career in pursuit of a calling that seeks to share God's transformative love and grace with the world. It is a vivid narrative of transformation—a quest to discover my place within the intricate tapestry of God's grand design. Through this account, I aim to highlight the enduring power of love—a force capable of illuminating even the darkest of paths and guiding us toward a brighter future.

CHAPTER 1

Navigating Early Uncertainties

Psalm 27:10 (NKJV)

"When my father and my mother forsake me, then the Lord will take care of me."

Chapter 1: Navigating Early Uncertainties

The world around me was a hazy blur, a canvas painted in countless shades of grey, where details drifted like wisps of smoke. My earliest memories are wrapped in a gentle fog reminiscent of the early morning mist that hangs heavily on the ground, softening the landscape and distorting the outlines of what is real. My parents existed as distant figures, almost ghostly apparitions in the periphery of my childhood life. They were present in body yet emotionally absent; they felt more like a faint whisper lost in the stillness of my early existence rather than the firm grounding one expects from parents.

My mother, Elizabeth Adeyemi Olofin (nee Adeleimu), was a teenager when the reality of pregnancy changed the course of her life forever. Initially, I was allowed to call her "Aunty," a name that now seems ironic considering the intriguing secret waiting to be uncovered. In her late teens, she found herself pregnant, a pivotal moment that echoed both promise and chaos. Envision a young woman, vibrant with hopes and dreams for her future, suddenly thrust into a world of overwhelming uncertainty. Navigating the complexities of adolescence while facing the impending responsibilities of motherhood must have created a whirlwind of thoughts within her. "Should I keep this child and face my parents, or should I seek a more discreet solution?" The weight of these questions must have pressed heavily upon her heart, each potential choice bearing grave consequences.

In a society where the stigma of unwed motherhood loomed like a dark cloud, the fear of social ostracism was pervasive. The pressures of tradition and expectations hit her hard. While many possibilities stretched before her, the fear of shame and judgement likely loomed larger. Ultimately, she chose to embrace the pregnancy, a choice that would permanently change her life. During that era, it was uncommon for parents to encourage their daughters to pursue higher education beyond primary school. Young women were often groomed for marriage and the management of households rather than scholarly achievement. Yet, my mother, with her inherent intelligence and athletic prowess, particularly in netball, was a rare exception. Her commendable grades and talents allowed her to attend a teacher-training college, a golden opportunity upended by the unexpected pregnancy she now bore.

The father of my unborn self, Chief Johnson Akinola Akomolode, was the young man my mother referred to as her first love. Their romance, initially filled with youthful exuberance and hope, quickly soured into a painful ordeal once the news of her pregnancy reached the families involved. The demands of culture and tradition descended upon them like a heavy shroud. My biological father, for reasons known only to him—whether fear of responsibility, immaturity, or peer pressure—denied all responsibilities related to the pregnancy. Such denial would prove to be a decision laden with regret. To me,

Chapter 1: Navigating Early Uncertainties

this act remains one of the most unfathomable tragedies; to deny an unborn child is not merely a moral failing but also constitutes a serious neglect of the potential life that could contribute to society.

Faced with the irrefutable reality of a child gestating within her and buoyed by the unwavering support of her parents, I entered the world on December 18, 1958. Following my birth, an informal yet crucial arrangement transpired: my grandparents, Pa Michael Adeleimu and Ma Atinuke Adeleimu, would assume full custody of me. This decision was designed to ensure my mother could continue her education uninterrupted. Thus, I was raised by my grandparents in Ikere-Ekiti, the second-largest town in Ekiti State, Western Nigeria, under the illusion that they were indeed my biological parents.

My grandfather was a multi-faceted figure within our community: an idol worshipper, a priest, a herbalist, and a skilled hunter, often referred to as "Ode." His charisma and command earned him a respected status, revered for his remarkable ability to remedy various ailments with the plants and herbs he meticulously cultivated. In a dim corner of the living room stood a figurine—a statue representing his worship—while behind his bedroom, a small enclosed garden echoed the whispers of nature, where he nurtured his herbal treasures. This sacred space was a domain where no soul dared venture apart from me, his favourite, lovingly nicknamed "Omo Baba."

Our bond was profound, a relationship characterised by intimacy and understanding, woven with threads of love and mutual respect.

We created countless memories: shared hunting trips into the forest, evenings immersed in storytelling under the moonlight, and whispers of laughter that echoed through the trees. Long, arduous treks often preceded our adventures, but my grandfather would lovingly scoop me onto his strong shoulders, transforming a tiring journey into a magical experience. At day's end, we would stretch out on beds of soft banana leaves, surrounded by the sounds of nature—a joyful connection to the earth rather than a sense of suffering.

My grandparents were firmly entrenched in their beliefs, having cultivated a life centred around idolatry, oblivious to the illuminating grace of Christ. My upbringing in this environment indoctrinated me into their worldviews, and I was perceived as the destined custodian of their idol, groomed for a future role as the priest one day. Yet destiny had other plans, as the Almighty God had a higher purpose waiting for me beyond the confines of that life. My grandparents, "Baba" and "Iya," as I affectionately called them, became the steadfast pillars of my early life, their love and unyielding lighthouse guiding me through the turbulent seas of childhood.

Chapter 1: Navigating Early Uncertainties

Grandson on grandfather's shoulder walking into the forest.

As time moved forward, my world changed dramatically when my Grandma passed away, followed by my Grandpa just a few months later. It was 1967, and I was only nine years old. Their absence opened a new chapter in my life, filled with uncertainty and unfamiliar paths. The warmth and love they had bestowed upon me left deep imprints on my heart. Yet, their loss also ignited a restless curiosity that would grow over the years—a deep, unquenchable desire for the unique affection that was once bestowed upon me.

In the wake of their passing, my mind became a flurry of questions, like autumn leaves swirling through the air. *Who would care for me?* I pondered. This quest for understanding became a driving force in my early life, steeped in longing and hope. Every year, my struggle to understand and accept their absence grew, creating a complex problem without clear answers. I wanted more than just knowledge; I craved a deep connection with those who had greatly impacted my life.

These questions created an unrelenting wave that occasionally overwhelmed me with their intensity as I navigated through childhood and adolescence. My journey was far from easy; it was peppered with challenges that tested my resilience. I faced rejection from people I reached out to, often encountering cruel words and inappropriate names that left scars on my self-esteem.

The hardships were many, and they weighed heavily on my young heart.

However, this trek was not devoid of triumphs. Each small victory in my pursuit of answers provided brief solace amidst the chaos. It was a painful pilgrimage through valleys of uncertainty, yet it was also a journey steeped in self-discovery. As I sought to uncover the hidden truths about grief and loss, I gradually began to understand myself better. I was piecing together my ancestry and forging a stronger sense of identity. With each revelation, I found empowerment in claiming my roots—my unique story—shaping me into the person I was destined to become.

CHAPTER 2

Charting A New Course

Psalm 23:4 (NIV)

"Even though I walk through the darkest valley, I will fear no evil, for you are with me; your rod and your staff, they comfort me."

Chapter 2: Charting A New Course

Life can sometimes lead us down unexpected paths and spark experiences we never imagined. Even if the idea initially appears overwhelming, a journey always starts with one step. I found myself at such a crossroads when the decision was made to uproot my life and relocate me to Ado-Ekiti, a place that existed only in the stories of others and was foreign to my own experiences. This transition was not just a physical move but an incredible learning, growth, and discovery opportunity. Little did I know that this journey would be pivotal in uncovering my true identity.

Once the decision was made, I was informed that I would live with a woman whom I had affectionately called Aunty during her occasional visits to Ikere-Ekiti. This choice was deemed the most suitable for my well-being, and my family was optimistic it would be a nurturing environment. I approached the idea excitedly, looking forward to the new experiences awaiting, especially given my aunt's history of bringing delightful gifts—ranging from colourful footballs to sweet treats—whenever she visited.

I arrived in Ado-Ekiti in 1967, at a time when the country was on the brink of chaos. The Nigerian government had declared war against the Republic of Biafra, plunging the nation into conflict. The civil war persisted for thirty gruelling months, culminating in Biafra's surrender on January 15, 1970. As a child, my recollections of this tumultuous period were characterised primarily by the pervasive unease that enveloped the atmosphere. The frightening backdrop of war was softened only by the comforting presence of my loving and supportive new family. My young age shielded me from the full gravity of the destruction and loss of lives that the civil war wrought.

My aunt, a dedicated primary school teacher, had created a relatively modern family milieu. She was married and had two children—my half-siblings— and housekeepers who helped manage their bustling household. However, the adjustment to this new family dynamic was anything but easy. Within a few weeks, I found adapting to their structured life increasingly challenging. The etiquette, mannerisms, and overall behaviour drastically differed from what I had been accustomed to. In my previous home, I had lived freely, with my grandfather allowing me to roam unencumbered. He was a man of few rules and had no qualms about defending my autonomy against any attempts at discipline. In stark contrast, my aunt's household adhered to a strict routine, and I was quickly out of my depth.

While such cultural adjustments can be common for anyone moving to a new environment, little did I realise I would feel alienated. My behaviour, which my family had always found endearing, was widely deemed unacceptable. I quickly felt out of place and struggled to fit in. A new arrangement was implemented to restore harmony: the esteemed family member we affectionately called "Iya-Irona" stepped into my life. Her real name was Marian Adeleimu, my great-aunt, who resided in another part of the town known as Irona. Out of deep respect, we consistently referred to her as Iya-Irona.

Iya-Irona's arrival in my life marked a heartwarming change. She served as my primary caregiver and emerged as a second mother, mentor, and a force of nature in my life. Her unwavering support and comfort became foundational throughout my transition. Iya-Irona possessed an innate understanding of my background, and she offered guidance as I navigated this unfamiliar, disciplined lifestyle. Though I continued to visit my aunt's family, where I grappled with my sense of belonging, it was with Iya-Irona that I found solace and a semblance of safety.

Living with Iya-Irona filled my days with emotional support, laughter, and comfort during life's inevitable ups and downs. She had a remarkable talent for offering guidance when I felt lost and was always ready to provide a shoulder to cry on. Yet her contributions weren't limited to emotional support—she was also a living repository of invaluable life lessons. And let's not overlook the culinary magic she worked in the kitchen; her cooking was exquisite. Each meal was enjoyable and tasty.

As time passed, two years slipped by in the blink of an eye. By the time I was preparing to enter Year 5 in primary school, I began to notice significant changes in my character. The initial longing for my grandparents had started to fade, overshadowed by a growing belief that they were no longer part of my life. Consequently, my aunt decided to make my stay with her a permanent arrangement, integrating me fully with the other children. However, this decision also unwittingly set the stage for unearthing a long-buried family secret.

People in our community referred to my aunty as "Eyelofin." At home, she was affectionately called "Mummy" by everyone except me. This peculiar custom began to influence me, and by the time I turned eleven, I found myself addressing her as a mummy for the first time, following the example set by the other kids. Until that moment, it had never fully settled in my mind that she was my biological mother. When I finally called her mummy, a warm smile spread across her face, and with lighthearted curiosity, she asked, "Who taught you to say that?" I shrugged and replied, "Just imitating everyone."

In the year 1969, our family joyously welcomed a beautiful baby boy. One typical evening, like countless others spent playing football with the neighbourhood kids, we gathered on a dusty field, kicking the ball around barefoot. It was a scene filled with infectious energy and the unrestrained laughter of childhood. Despite the

Chapter 2: Charting A New Course

imperfections of the field, we relished every moment under the blazing sun, which cast long, dramatic shadows over our makeshift playing area. As fatigue set in, our thirst grew, and one by one, we made our way to find something to drink.

A vibrant scene depicting young boys playing football.

In my haste, I dashed into the house, grabbed a cup of a seemingly innocuous "white" drink sitting on the table, and drank it in quick gulps. My mother was present, cradling the baby in her arms, but she was caught off guard and couldn't stop me in time. Unbeknownst to me, what I had just consumed was expressed breast milk meant for the baby. The moment I finished, I noticed a subtle but profound change in her expression, one I couldn't quite decipher at the time.

She then called me into her bedroom, and with a serious yet gentle demeanour, she unfolded a heavy secret she had guarded for over a decade. Locking her gaze with mine, she said softly, "By the way, I am your biological mother. What you had just drunk was my breast milk—the first ever from me since you were born." This revelation seemed to lift a weight off her shoulders but left me bewildered and troubled. "Where and who is my father?" I asked in a rush of questions. "Your biological father passed away when you were just a baby," she replied, and beyond this, she offered no further details. That day, we didn't delve deeper into the matter; I sensed the burden it placed on her heart and felt no urge to contribute to her sorrow. Conversations regarding my father would come years later when I could better understand the complexity of our family dynamics.

By late 1972, my life took another significant turn as I was relocated to Lagos, the bustling capital of Nigeria

Chapter 2: Charting A New Course

Mother and son sharing a deep and heartfelt conversation.

at the time, to live with my first cousin, Theophilus Olujoka, whom I respectfully referred to as "Oga Theo." The reasons behind this sudden move were shrouded in mystery; I didn't dare ask why I was being taken to Lagos. I was simply told, "You are going to Lagos." Reflecting on it much later, I realised that this decision was likely driven by our family's financial constraints and the growing challenges we faced.

As a primary school teacher, my mother's salary was meagre; sometimes, her wages would be delayed or unpaid for several months. Our family size had expanded by this period, yet my stepfather had become increasingly distant and unsupportive. He contributed little to the household or the children's education, leaving my mother to shoulder practically all the responsibilities. Despite the mounting challenges, she bore them with remarkable strength and determination, striving to provide the best for us within the confines of her limited means, even as certain necessities remained tantalisingly out of reach.

I began my journey through secondary school in Lagos in 1974, enrolling at the prestigious Baptist Academy. Before this pivotal moment, I was known simply as Gbenga George, a straightforward combination of my first and middle names. However, during the registration process in school, my first cousin took the liberty of formalising my name as Gbenga George Adeyemi, integrating Adeyemi, which I later found out was my mother's middle name. The omission of my father's name was a perplexing detail that reflected the complexities of my story. In an era where questioning adults was seen as impolite and disrespectful, I accepted the change without further inquiry, even though it left me with lingering questions.

My time in Lagos was quite brief. Just weeks after completing my first year at Baptist Academy, I was on a packed public bus returning to Ado-Ekiti. The recent marriage of my first cousin altered our living arrangements, making my continued stay unfeasible. More pressing for my mother was her deep concern for my safety; she wanted to shield me from the influence of gangs and criminal activities that were rampant in the city. Years later, I would understand the full extent of her concerns.

Lagos, a city bustling with excellence and vibrancy, was also laden with stress and high living costs. It offered an array of attractions and opportunities yet also bore witness to disturbingly high levels of violent crime. I often reminisce about the social cohesion and the pulsating lifestyle that the city provided, aspects I found immensely appealing, even if my experiences there were short-lived.

Reflecting on my stepfather brings forth a sensitive and complex narrative. Chief Festus Olofin had many admirable qualities: clever, handsome, hardworking, and intelligent. However, these attributes were overshadowed by a darker side characterised by unloving behaviour, alcoholism, womanising, and violent tendencies. The family, which had once been admired and envied in the community, gradually descended into a whirlwind of turmoil and distress. My mother was at a loss, struggling to navigate the drastic changes in the man she had married. It felt as though every member of the family had their own experiences of his concerning behaviours, including instances of physical violence directed at our mother. The absence of joy and laughter in our home became palpable when he was present.

One particularly painful moment was when he called me a "bastard," a comment that deeply wounded my mother. Cultural and traditional norms often made holding him accountable for his actions virtually impossible, as they played to his advantage. Nevertheless, before his passing in 2000, I found an opportunity to confront some lingering issues between us. During those discussions, I earnestly pleaded with him to repair his relationships with his children, a conversation that remains etched in my memory.

Recognising that regardless of the trials you face within your family, you are not isolated in your struggles is vital. Many individuals have traversed similar pathways, and reaching out for support can be immensely beneficial. The truth can often be painful, yet it has the potential to offer closure and pave the way for healing. I've come to appreciate that my journey is not merely a tragedy but a testament to the resilience of the human spirit. My mother always believed that love and faith could endure through even the most overwhelming challenges.

The lessons gleaned from these experiences have proven invaluable. They illuminated the complexities of familial relationships, love's transformative power, and forgiveness's importance. My faith has also been fortified, instilling in me the belief that divine grace can touch the darkest corners of existence.

As I navigated the intricate maze of my past, I felt an undeniable pull toward the comforting embrace of my Heavenly Father, the Almighty God. The scripture verses became a source of solace and peace, offering quietude amid the emotional tumult. A strong anchor that helped me navigate the transition into adulthood was also provided by my mother's and my great-aunt's constant support and their significant sacrifices. Their love fortified me, making me stronger and more resilient in adversity.

CHAPTER 3

Establishing Strong Foundations

Deuteronomy 33:26 (NIV)

"There is no one like the God of Jeshurun, who rides across the heavens to help you and on the clouds in his majesty."

The fog of navigating a new path began to lift, revealing a profound sense of incomplete identity that I couldn't quite articulate. My grandparents, those steadfast pillars of love and support in my life, cultivated in me a deep-seated thirst for family and belonging. They were remarkable symbols of resilience and unwavering determination, embodying the notion that hard work and unity were paramount. Under their nurturing guidance, I began my primary school education in 1965 at the tender age of seven.

Back then, primary education in the Western Region of Nigeria was free, a beacon of hope for many families striving for a better future. The curriculum encompassed general subjects, including reading, arithmetic, and communication skills. Initially, students learned in their local dialect, a testament to the value placed on cultural roots, before transitioning to English in the fourth year. This foundational stage culminated in the awarding of a Primary School Leaving Certificate, a significant milestone for every child.

Despite the challenges of growing up in a household that often faced shortages of necessities and an overall life that could be described as below average, my experience in the academic world painted a different picture. Throughout my educational journey—from early childhood through primary and into secondary and tertiary education—I consistently excelled, frequently ranking among the top three students in the class. Teachers recognised my potential, labelling me as one of the most gifted and talented pupils. This acclaim led to my advanced year in primary and secondary school, a testament to my work ethic and intellectual curiosity. I was a true "Philomath," possessing an insatiable passion for learning and discovery.

Upon returning from the bustling city of Lagos, I joined Methodist Comprehensive High School (MCHS) in Aaye-Ekiti, a co-educational boarding school nestled in a quiet rural village. The simplicity of village life was a stark contrast to Lagos's vibrant urban culture. MCHS was a newly established institution, and its facilities and standards were markedly different from the more established Baptist Academy I had attended in Lagos. Recognising my impressive academic results, the principal decided to fast-track my progression, placing me directly in Year 3 instead of Year 2.

At MCHS, discipline, manual labour, and the importance of physical activity were core tenets ingrained deeply in the minds and hearts of the students through both instruction and daily practice. Life at the school was challenging yet transformative; these experiences, though rigorous and demanding, served to equip us for the complexities of life beyond the classroom. Each trial moulded us into resilient individuals, preparing us not only academically but also for the future we aspired to build.

My journey through education has been marked by a series of unforgettable experiences that began in my early school days. By the time I reached Year 4 of secondary school, I had already earned a reputation among my immediate seniors. This branding was not merely a matter of recognition; it stemmed from my frequent encounters with a particularly challenging subject—mathematics. Whenever the class struggled to solve complex problems, the teacher often called on me to provide the answers. While this may have seemed like an honour, it came with unintended consequences that turned my school life into a precarious balancing act.

The praise from the teacher was met with resentment from my seniors, who felt overshadowed and humiliated by my presence. Their anger manifested in various ways, often waiting for me outside the classroom to administer punishment, which typically included both physical beatings and demanding manual labour. They perceived my success as a source of disgrace for themselves, and I quickly learned to navigate this toxic dynamic. I adopted a self-preservation strategy to shield myself from their wrath: feign ignorance whenever the teacher called upon me. This manoeuvre allowed me to escape the repercussions of my earlier successes, restoring a semblance of normalcy to my daily life.

By 1978, I reached a significant milestone when I completed the West Africa Secondary School Leaving Certificate Examination (WAEC) with outstanding results. My grades distinguished me within my school and set a record in the entire region. The pride radiating from my mother during this moment was indescribable; her joy was palpable, illuminating her face with an expression I'd rarely seen before. This achievement paved the way for my next educational venture—a two-year stint at Christ School, Ado-Ekiti, where I pursued the Higher School Certificate (HSC).

The pursuit of knowledge during this time was both enjoyable and demanding. This enjoyment stemmed from my insatiable curiosity and thirst for learning, while the demands primarily arose from the heavy financial burdens I faced. Despite these challenges, I was incredibly motivated to further my education at the prestigious University of Ife, Nigeria. This place felt worlds apart from the small town where I had grown up. The university campus was alive with intellectual energy—students engaged in discussions, debates, and explorations of ideas that made me feel enlivened and amongst like-minded individuals. It was a place where I could truly explore my passions and evolve.

Choosing my major was a complex decision driven by a blend of ambition and personal interest rather than practicality. I opted for engineering physics, a relatively new and underexplored field many seemed to avoid. I was drawn to the idea that it could elevate me into prominence, leading to opportunities that had previously felt out of reach. However, this journey was intertwined with a significant setback: the ever-looming financial strain that dictated my life as a student. Without the means to purchase textbooks, I often grappled with a lack of essential resources. My living situation was far from ideal; I frequently slept in locations that were less than comfortable, as I could not afford the necessary accommodation fees. Food insecurity became a constant companion, my stomach often echoing the struggles I faced. During this turbulent time, a part of me yearned for support, for fatherly guidance, as everything around me felt increasingly dark and overwhelming.

Undeterred by these challenges, I was driven by my ambition and an intense desire to prove myself. I dove deep into my studies, fully immersing myself in coursework. This dedication paid off—it wasn't just about getting by; I excelled in my classes, earning praise and admiration from my tutors and peers. I found myself continuously pushed beyond the boundaries of my comfort zone. This environment challenged me to think critically, engage deeply with the material, and strive relentlessly for excellence.

My passion for learning was so profound that I developed a remarkable memorisation technique, which earned me the nickname "The Working Library." This moniker reflected my unique habit: whenever I borrowed a textbook from the library or fellow students, I made it my mission to memorise its entire contents. This intensive approach to learning not only solidified my understanding of complex subjects but also transformed the learning experience into a personal triumph. With time, I discovered a rhythm—a satisfying sense of accomplishment from mastering difficult concepts and a newfound confidence that propelled me forward.

In my first year at university, I was fortunate to have secured accommodation, which felt like a blessing. However, as I progressed into my second and third years, that luxury became a distant memory; financial constraints meant that affording a place to stay was no longer viable. The reality was stark: I had no money to pay for housing. This situation dramatically affected where I could sleep at night. Rather than succumb to despair, I found resourceful ways to cope. I adopted a routine that involved alternating between a desk in the library for studying and resting, and a bench in the canteen of a residence hall. Today, we might refer to this as rough sleeping, but quitting was never an option for someone with a resilient heart during those tough times.

The university canteen followed what I learned as the "1-1-1" pattern for meals, which stands for breakfast, lunch, and dinner. Many students around me who had

Chapter 3: Establishing Strong Foundations

the means comfortably fell into this routine, relishing the availability of three meals each day. My circumstances, however, placed me in a more precarious category—one where I could only afford one meal daily. Thus, I had to devise a careful strategy for nourishment. I often fluctuated between several meal plans: sometimes "1-0-0," occasionally "0-1-0," or even "0-0-1," depending on which meal would provide the essential calories to sustain me throughout the day. It was undeniably challenging, but I believed there would be rewards for my perseverance.

Life, I learned, is not a straight path. The journey is fraught with bumps and unexpected turns, each presenting its own set of painful experiences. The race toward personal growth and success is tangible and sometimes brutally demanding. However, I learned that none of these struggles should define who we are or can become. Disappointments are a part of life, but I firmly held onto the belief that discouragement is a choice, which I vehemently rejected. I chose not to be discouraged or let the hardships diminish my ambition or drive.

Graduation day arrived—a moment of triumph, a culmination of three years filled with hard work, dedication, and sacrifice. As I clutched my degree certificate, the weight of achievement settled on my shoulders. It was a first-class honour, a tangible symbol of resilience, perseverance, and accomplishment, and it stood as a testament to the countless sacrifices my mother had made to see me through this journey. The celebrations in our neighbourhood erupted like fireworks—joyful shouts and laughter filled the air as we returned home from the graduation ceremony. This collective euphoria around my remarkable achievement lingered for days, enveloping me with pride. Yet, intertwined with this joy was a bittersweet realisation: while I had reached a significant milestone, the real world was waiting just beyond the horizon.

The prospect of stepping into the real world felt both thrilling and daunting. I could barely contain my excitement to embark on this new chapter of my life. In 1984, I secured my first job at the Centre for Energy Research and Training (CERT) at Ahmadu Bello University (ABU) in Zaria, northern Nigeria. I was appointed as a Graduate Assistant—a role that represented a crucial stepping stone towards a brighter future. It was the academic environment I had always longed for, a space where I felt at home amidst intellectual fervour. The fact that this opportunity came to me without needing a formal application or an interview was surreal. The university had been tracking my academic progress from the very beginning, and they could hardly wait for my National Youth Service Corps (NYSC) completion before posting a job offer. The NYSC is a mandatory scheme designed to foster common ties and promote national unity among the youth. I couldn't help but feel that a higher power was at work behind the scenes—perhaps it was divine favour orchestrated by my Heavenly Father.

Another significant milestone unfolded in 1986. Navigating a career path as a non-Muslim and non-indigene at a university in Northern Nigeria was often a daunting task. The region faced an educational crisis, as it remained significantly poorer academically than its southern counterpart. Historical factors contributed to this educational gap, with cultural and religious attitudes in the North traditionally less supportive of education. However, strides have been made to bridge this divide. I was fortunate to be selected among six individuals for a postgraduate study programme abroad—a result of a planned intervention aimed at transforming literacy levels and educational opportunities for Indigenous students.

In August 1986, I arrived in the UK from Nigeria during a heavy snowstorm to start my PhD in Medical Physics at the University of Aberdeen. The landscape was stunning, covered in a pristine white blanket that created a picturesque and tranquil setting. Experiencing snow for the first time felt like stepping into a scene from a movie, but the chill quickly took hold. Walking through the deep snow was tough, and my toes soon got cold, even with warm clothing. My initial excitement faded as students were advised to remain indoors, and I regretted not being better equipped for the harsh weather—lacking a winter coat and proper footwear.

Nonetheless, the thrill of immersing myself in a new culture and pursuing advanced studies fueled my determination and optimism. As the days passed, I adjusted my wardrobe, adding a thermal jacket, neck scarf, hat, and gloves. Studying in Aberdeen was a pivotal decision, and I remain hopeful that things will get easier.

Unfortunately, this optimism waned when, during my second year, ABU unexpectedly retracted its commitment to support my education financially. Despite this setback, I persevered and completed my PhD in Medical Physics at Aberdeen University in the United Kingdom in 1991, with partial assistance from alternative funding sources and the unwavering support of my wife.

The attainment of a PhD opened doors to a thirty-year career with the UK National Health Service (NHS). The journey was not without its challenges; it was replete with uncertainties and hurdles that tested my resolve. Yet, despite the pressures and demands of the role, I felt an unquenchable yearning for something more—something that would propel me further along my path. My position as the Head of Radiotherapy Physics within the NHS came with its unique challenges: long hours, arduous tasks, and the relentless pressure to meet increasingly unrealistic targets began to weigh heavily on me. Each day blended in a relentless grind, leaving me emotionally exhausted and questioning whether this was how I wanted to live out the remainder of my life.

As I climbed the professional ladder, the thought of leaving the NHS filled me with trepidation. I had devoted years to building a successful career and establishing a level of financial security that many would envy. But I often grappled with deep-seated questions: Was I truly ready to abandon this path I had worked so hard to carve for myself? Could I envision a different existence outside the confines of the NHS? The uncertainty stirred within me, leaving me unsettled and searching for satisfying answers that remained just out of reach.

As time passed, a subtle sense of dissatisfaction began to creep in beneath the veneer of professional success. It wasn't about the financial gains or the prestige associated with my role; instead, it manifested as a persistent gnawing feeling that something essential was still amiss. What could it possibly be?

CHAPTER 4

Impressions That Endure

Psalm 103:2 (NIV)

"Praise the Lord, my soul, and forget not all his benefits."

Chapter 4: Impressions That Endure

When I reflect on some of the most important moments in my life, some memories come back to me with remarkable clarity, frequently because they are meaningful and have had a long-lasting effect. These experiences are etched deeply in my heart, which is why they have stayed with me ever since they occurred.

One such defining moment occurred in early 1979 during my second year of HSC A/L at Christ School, Ado-Ekiti. It was a time of youthful aspirations and dreams for the future, but it also became a crucial learning experience that would shape my understanding of actions, responsibilities and consequences. I learned a vital lesson that would resonate throughout my life. In legal terms, the principle of *"ignorantia juris non excusat,"* or *"ignorance of the law excuses not,"* underscores that being unaware of a law does not exempt one from its penalties.

The events began when a senior secondary schoolmate, who had finished a year ahead of me from Methodist Comprehensive High School, found himself in a precarious situation. He had attempted the West African Examination Council (WAEC) exams twice but failed. In desperation, he approached me, asking for a favour: to sit for the exam on his behalf. Initially hesitant, I succumbed to his persistent appeals and pressure, ultimately agreeing to his request. I misguidedly believed

I was simply being a supportive friend, offering a helping hand. Little did I know that my willingness to assist would put me in direct violation of the law.

Now, I have completed seven out of eight registered subjects and was prepared to take the exam for the eighth subject on the final exam day. On this day, the gravity of our actions became starkly apparent when both of us foolishly walked into the exam hall. We were apprehended and taken into police custody, our future hanging precariously in the balance. Spending a night in a small, dark, empty, filthy police cell was a suffocating experience I wouldn't wish on anyone. The moment the metal door clanged shut behind me, the harsh reality of lost freedom hit hard. The following day, we found ourselves standing before a stern magistrate, where the charges of conspiracy and impersonation were brought against us. The maximum penalty for each charge was seven years, and the magistrate's judgement was the only factor determining whether they might be prosecuted simultaneously. At that moment, I felt an overwhelming sense of despair and hopelessness, as if my entire life was crumbling before me.

As weeks passed, the court proceedings unfolded. I was engulfed in a whirlwind of anxiety and uncertainty, waiting for the final verdict. The day arrived when both the sentencing and the verdict would be delivered, and my heart raced with dread and trepidation. Out of nowhere,

Chapter 4: Impressions That Endure

as if shielded by a higher power, the magistrate issued an unprecedented ruling—an absolute discharge. We were released unconditionally, without any penalties. Our legal representatives later informed us that this was one of the most lenient sentences ever delivered by that magistrate. At that moment, a wave of relief washed over me. It felt like a second chance to continue my education and pursue my dreams.

Throughout this tumultuous experience, my mother stood as my unwavering pillar of strength. Her faith and encouragement were constant sources of comfort. Every night filled with anxiety and sleeplessness was met with her prophetic reassurances that everything would turn out fine. Her unconditional support and belief in me made her my unsung hero during those trying times.

Unsung heroes truly surround us in everyday life, often unrecognised and overlooked. They come in various forms, doing remarkable things without seeking the spotlight. Even without fame or fortune, their impacts leave indelible marks on the lives of those around them. Unlike fictional superheroes with extraordinary abilities, these real-life champions may not appear in comic books or movies, but their contributions are just as significant. They teach us valuable lessons, shaping our character and guiding us through our darkest moments. Their quiet resilience and strength remind us that true heroism often lies in simple acts of kindness and unwavering support amidst the chaos of life.

These unsung heroes leave lasting impressions on our lives through their sacrifices, kindness, hard work, and unwavering support. They are the ones who teach us, inspire us, make us laugh, give us hope, and guide us through life's challenges. They exemplify strength, kindness, and resilience. Among these remarkable individuals, I want to highlight three women who have profoundly impacted my life, leaving indelible marks that nothing can erase.

The first is my mother, affectionately known by many as "Eyelofin." She truly embodies the spirit of an unsung hero, deserving of deep appreciation for her selfless actions. As a mother of five, she was a rare gem, tirelessly investing in each of us with the little resources she had. Her life was filled with sacrifices, particularly concerning our education. Beyond her children, her compassion extended to many who crossed her path; each of them has a unique story of how she touched their lives.

I distinctly remember her as a woman overflowing with love and charm, radiating warmth that enveloped everyone around her. A skilled artisan, she excelled in handiwork, especially in dressmaking and hairmaking, showcasing many talents. I learned invaluable practical skills from her—sewing, hairstyling, cooking, and the importance of endurance in the face of life's challenges. Unfortunately, over the years, the pressures of life took a toll on her health, leading to medical struggles that spanned two decades until her passing in 2015. Her courage, through all her hardships, was nothing short of phenomenal.

The second woman I wish to honour is my great aunt, whom we affectionately called "Iya-Irona." Her bravery and determination make her an unsung hero in my life, especially for the incident in 1970 when I was just twelve years old and in Year 5 at primary school. During our annual sports event preparations, the school assigned students to gather wood logs and palm leaves from the nearby forest. After classes, a group of friends and I ventured deep into the woods, carefree and excited about our task.

Suddenly, we faced a terrifying situation when a fierce-looking man appeared, causing us to panic and scatter in various directions. In the chaos, I found myself lost and completely disoriented. I frantically called out for my friends, my voice echoing in the silence, but there was no response. It was as if the forest had swallowed them whole, and a creeping fear began to grip my heart. As the sun dipped below the horizon and darkness enveloped the woods, I realised the gravity of my situation—I was utterly lost.

The experience of being lost in a forest is a harrowing memory that remains etched in my mind. As night descended, my great aunt sensed something was amiss. I should have been home long ago. Gathering a few supportive neighbours, she organised a search in our small community, where formal search teams were nonexistent. They scoured the area, their concern palpable as hours stretched painfully on. Eventually, they reconvened at the "old garage," a dilapidated structure that served as a landmark in our town.

Most of the neighbours had to leave as dusk turned night, but my great-aunt was undeterred. She refused to go home, choosing instead to stay at the old garage all night, willing to risk her safety. Her heart was heavy with worry, but she held onto hope, remaining steadfast in her resolve to find me.

Through unforeseen help, I found my way out of the forest to a dusty rural road. Just as despair began to set in, a flickering light appeared in the distance. It was a farmer and his family returning home after a long day of work. They were astonished to find me alone on the roadside at such an hour. I shared my tale with them, and they graciously took me back to the heart of the town, where I was joyfully reunited with my great aunt. Her expression was a blend of relief and delight, tears of joy streaming down her face as she embraced me, knowing I was finally safe.

Chapter 4: Impressions That Endure

Great-aunt sitting on the kerb in a quaint old town centre.

When we arrived home in the early morning hours, she lovingly prepared a meal for me, tending to my needs with a tenderness that only she could provide. I was so weary from the ordeal that I immediately fell asleep, comforted by her presence and care. She was an admirable woman—her bravery and unconditional love during that traumatic episode will forever remain in my heart.

Another admirable woman who holds a special place in my heart is my wife, Olabimpe, who is truly one of my unsung heroes. Her story is a deeply heartwarming one, illustrating the incredible sacrifices she has made for our family. She has been my unwavering support throughout my academic journey, and I would not have reached this point without her steadfast presence by my side.

During a particularly challenging phase of my life, she made the selfless decision to take our family's financial responsibility. This choice came during unexpected financial turmoil when my scholarship was abruptly rescinded. In my second year of PhD studies, I could not secure additional funding, which posed a serious threat to my aspirations of completing the post-doctorate degree. It was a time fraught with uncertainty, and the fear of my dreams slipping away loomed large.

However, Olabimpe's incredible resolve and unwavering commitment shone through. She balanced

Chapter 4: Impressions That Endure

multiple odd jobs, working late hours and managing household responsibilities while encouraging me to persevere. Her sacrifices supported me financially and provided a strong emotional backbone during those trying times. On my graduation day, her pride was palpable, not just for the degree I had earned but for the fruitful investment she had made in my future.

Olabimpe's contributions extend beyond practical support; she has played a pivotal role in shaping my personal and professional growth. Her love and encouragement have consistently motivated me, driving me toward success. She had a cherished Yoruba proverb she would whisper to encourage me: *"Òtítọ́ náà pé ẹṣin ju ẹni tí ó gùn ún sọ̀ kalẹ̀ kò dá ẹni tí ó gùn ún dúró láti dìde kí ó sì tún gun ún."* It translates to "The fact that the horse throws down the rider does not prevent the rider from getting up and mounting again." It means "Never give up," a mantra she embodied throughout my PhD journey.

Reflecting on my life, I realise that my unsung heroes have served as antidotes to my despair—individuals God has placed in my life for a reason. Above all, I acknowledge the role of my Heavenly Father, the Almighty God. He has promised never to abandon me, guiding me even through the darkest valleys of life, and ultimately knows and controls the future. Another Yoruba proverb that resonates with this sentiment: *"Omi tí ènìyàn bá yàn láti mu kò ní ṣàn kọjá ọkan."* It translates to "The water that one is destined to drink will never flow past one," reminding me that whatever is meant for me will come to pass.

In contemplating my Heavenly Father, I also recall a significant piece of my puzzle that I thought would remain forever elusive: my family roots. For years, I had been told that my biological father had passed away when I was just a baby, but details surrounding his ancestry were shrouded in mystery. I lacked basic information about him—his name, where he lived or was born, and the dates of his birth or demise. This identity gap weighed heavily on me; I needed to know who I truly was and from whom I inherited my traits. Strangely, discussing this topic seemed taboo, as if everyone around me had taken an unspoken vow of secrecy.

Then, one evening in 1997, something happened that seemed like fate. After a particularly demanding workday, I was fatigued and opted to watch television while slumped on the sofa. The day had drained me physically, but the emotional weight of my unanswered questions felt much heavier. My children had just returned from school, their youthful exuberance filling the room until they asked me a poignant question: "Daddy, why can't our grandparents come over to take us to school like the other children?"

In a moment of honesty tinged with sadness, I explained that Grandma was unable to visit due to severe health issues and that Grandpa had long passed away. While my children expressed disappointment, they also felt sympathy for my predicament. Hearing this conversation, my wife had just come in from the kitchen. With a surprising level of conviction, she informed me that my father was still alive.

At first, I dismissed her assertion, unable to fathom how she could be so sure. As my mother was still alive, I felt compelled to bring this conversation to her. After several exchanges filled with questions, the final piece of the puzzle finally surfaced. To my amazement, my mother confirmed that my father was indeed alive.

When I finally met my biological father for the first time at the age of forty, I found myself filled with a mix of preparation and uncertainty. It was a moment I had envisioned countless times—an opportunity to piece together my fragmented identity and connect with my roots. Meanwhile, during the years of intense financial pressure and hardship I endured, he had been living a comfortable life. He had forged a successful academic career and rose to the position of principal of a school before his retirement.

Despite our differences and the gap in our relationship, I approached our meeting from a place of love, forgiveness, and reconciliation rather than harbouring anger or resentment for his past absence. He was now in the winter of his life, and while I felt a deep-seated discontent regarding our lost years, my heart was open. Though I received a few quick responses to some of my long-held questions about why he had denied my pregnancy, many were far from satisfying. He shared that, at one point, he had been ready to reconnect, but my mother had not shown interest in encouraging that path.

My father had married and fathered five other children—three sons and two daughters. After spending many years teaching, he decided to retire and return to his hometown of Ikere-Ekiti, where I had grown up. Although he was my biological father, I had never truly experienced the essence of having a dad in my life, as he had largely been absent during my upbringing.

As I reflected on our relationship, I realised that we had a couple of decades worth of missed opportunities to bond and connect on a deeper level yet. Unfortunately, it never materialised. After a brief reunion, my father passed away in 2019, leaving behind a myriad of questions that I would never get answers to—questions that had been buried alongside him in the grave. My mother had also departed four years prior, adding to the weight of my loss.

Despite the pain of unanswered questions and the unresolved feelings that trailed behind me like shadows,

Chapter 4: Impressions That Endure

I found solace in honouring their lives through their burials. This act was not just a farewell but a celebration of who they were and their impact on my life. I was also grateful to meet my half-siblings, each of whom brought new dimensions to my understanding of family. Together, we started to piece our shared legacy, tracing a family tree that I could eventually share with my children.

The family tree focuses on immediate family members spanning four generations—two generations preceding my own and one generation succeeding. It encompasses my grandparents, parents, siblings, and their respective children. On my mother's side, her father was polygamous; however, he and my grandmother had a total of five children: three sons and two daughters, with my mother being the youngest of the siblings. Notably, I possess detailed lineage information for my maternal ancestry. Yet, I have been unable to garner more pertinent information regarding my paternal grandparents, leaving this aspect of heritage unresolved.

My family possesses a rich cultural background and distinct ethnic identity, which has rendered the research particularly significant. I have intentionally refrained from tracing the familial lines to include my siblings' spouses, recognising that doing so would further enhance the narrative of our family history. A particularly remarkable aspect of my lineage is that I am the firstborn on both sides of the family. This

Against All Odds

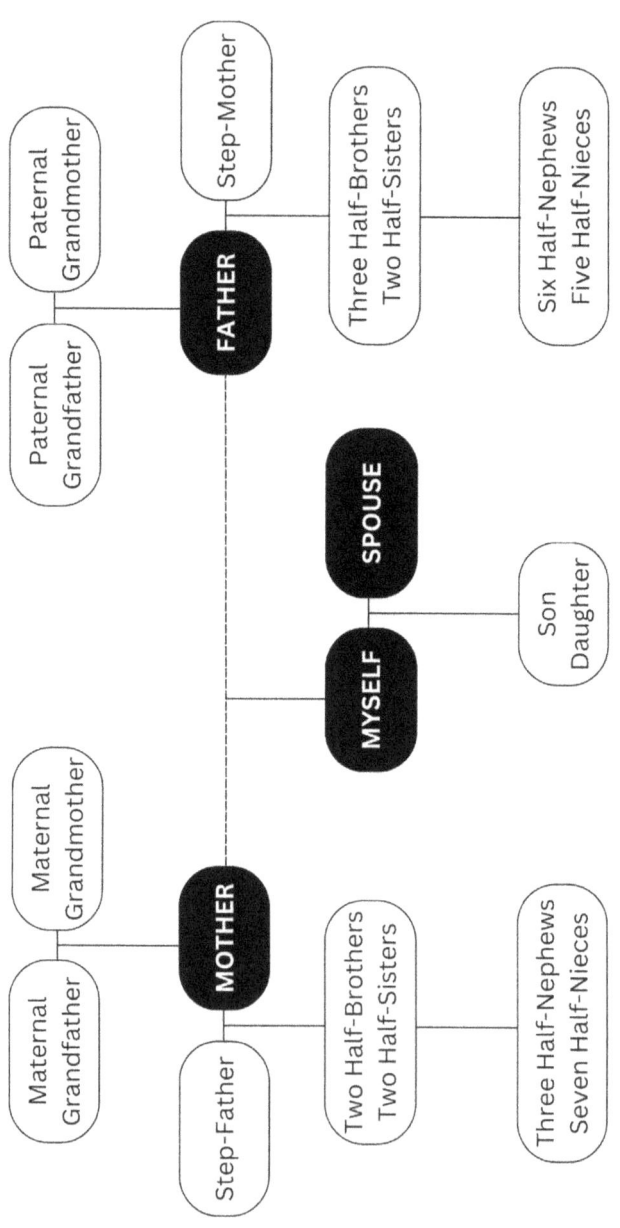

My family tree

position carries considerable expectations as I navigate the traditions and responsibilities transmitted through generations.

In many ways, this experience was like completing a complex puzzle. Some long-buried secrets about my lineage were finally unlocked, dispelling clouds of doubt and uncertainty that had loomed for so long. With this newfound clarity, I felt the seeds of a new chapter taking root in my life.

It's important to recognise that setbacks can occur in anyone's life, regardless of whether a father figure is present or absent. This reality shows that we can still achieve great things and succeed without using setbacks as reasons to stop moving forward. Before fully embracing the new chapter of life, I am compelled to take a brief detour to explore the significance of our inner anchors during times of adversity. These anchors help us navigate life's tumultuous waters, allowing us to rise above our circumstances and continue moving forward.

CHAPTER 5

The Inner Anchors

2 Peter 1:3 (NIV)

"His divine power has given us everything we need for a Godly life through our knowledge of Him who called us by His own glory and goodness."

Chapter 5: The Inner Anchors

The sun, a radiant orb shining brightly in a sky freshly cleansed by a recent downpour, cast soft, golden rays through my study window. Here I sat, immersed in contemplation, exploring the compelling statistics from the National Fatherhood Initiative regarding the crucial role fathers play in their children's lives *(reference https://www.fatherhood.org/father-absence-statistic)*. A cup of tea, now tepid and forgotten, lingered on my desk, a testament to the passage of time in my quiet sanctuary. Outside, a gentle breeze danced through the trees, providing a refreshing contrast to the day's heat, as nature orchestrated a symphony—a delicate blend of rustling leaves and distant birdcalls.

Amidst this serene backdrop, my thoughts drifted towards the impact of paternal absence. The data I had been analysing struck a poignant chord within me, illuminating the numerous unfortunate ways a father's absence can ripple through a child's life. Conversely, the presence of an involved father can significantly enhance the emotional and psychological well-being of both children and mothers. The overwhelming positive influence that engaged fathers provide cannot be understated, as it fosters stability and nurtures the development of resilient, well-rounded individuals.

Yet, as enlightening as these statistics may be, my journey adds depth to this conversation. It brings to light the paramount significance of cultivating our inner anchors. Children who grow up without their fathers often navigate a turbulent sea of challenges and emotional uncertainties, feeling like small boats tossed about in a relentless storm. An inner anchor represents that calm, steadfast essence within—capable of withstanding life's storms. With a strong inner anchor, one can glide through life's ups and downs, riding the waves with newfound confidence and strength.

The inner anchor is not merely a concept; it is a powerful voice reverberating within, reminding us of our inherent worth, unique strengths, and aspirational goals. It embodies our value system, faith, or creative pursuits that spark our imaginations. It stabilises during turbulent times, helping us stand firm as unexpected changes try to shake us. Cultivating resilience and adaptability becomes crucial, especially when our intrinsic qualities and talents, if nurtured early, serve as steadfast guides toward greatness and a hopeful future.

Reflecting on the years my father was absent, I realise that my grounding force was my unwavering passion for education. The love for learning imbued my life with purpose and direction, allowing me to navigate the chaotic waters of adolescence. My insatiable curiosity drove me to explore new ideas and perspectives, igniting a desire to embrace opportunities that came my way. The inner joy derived from education equipped me to transform challenges into stepping stones for personal growth.

For some, their inner anchors may manifest through a passion for sports, arts, music, or writings. However, it's essential to acknowledge that substances such as drugs, tobacco, and alcohol do not serve as genuine anchors. These are mere illusions—temporary distractions that numb our pain but ultimately fail to provide lasting support. They can't hold us steady against the overwhelming tides of hardship and setbacks; instead, they only offer a fleeting escape, a soft cover for our feelings before harsh reality re-emerges. True inner anchors stand firmly against the tides, providing essential stability and clarity, catalysing our refocus and resilience in the face of adversity.

For children who grow up without fathers or with absent fathers, the likelihood of achieving a successful life is often underestimated. Those chances are quite high! Being an example, I successfully earned a PhD and built a rewarding career in the healthcare sector, all without the presence of a father figure. My experience shows that anyone can carve out a meaningful existence if they cultivate the right motivation and ambition—what I like to call their "inner anchors."

Numerous successful individuals serve as a testament to this belief. Figures such as Steve Jobs, Pierce Brosnan,

Mariah Carey, Samuel L. Jackson, and the legendary jazz singer Ella Fitzgerald each navigated their journeys without the full support of one or both parents. Notably, American presidents like Gerald Ford, Bill Clinton, and Barack Obama lost their fathers during their formative years yet still achieved remarkable success. Their stories offer invaluable insights into overcoming adversity, and I encourage you to delve into them. Learning what fueled their drive can inspire you to foster the same resilience and determination in your life. Surrounding yourself with a positive support network is crucial. Seek out people who uplift, encourage, and challenge you to explore your potential. This camaraderie can act as a catalyst for personal growth and significantly enhance your journey toward success.

Discovering your inner anchor is transformative, requiring exploration, development, nourishment, and application. This process can take time and might necessitate a supportive community to help you identify and strengthen those anchors. Understanding the importance of these inner anchors can have profound implications for your life. While they may not prevent external storms or challenges, they can be a grounding force amidst life's upheavals.

The utility of your inner anchor extends beyond mere survival. It can help mitigate stress and anxiety, enhance your capacity for appropriate responses, and facilitate positive behavioural changes. Harnessing this inner strength is a powerful strategy to overcome adversity and propel you toward your life goals.

The concept of grounding has been essential to my identity and growth. The challenges I faced and the struggles I endured shaped me, refining my character and deepening my understanding of God's love. I learned that true strength doesn't lie in external accolades or material success but rather in an unwavering trust in a higher power.

The scripture *"The Lord is my shepherd; I shall not want"* from Psalm 23, once just a familiar phrase, now resonates deeply within my spirit. This truth, born out of personal experience, has been my sustenance through hardships, guiding and propelling me into a life dedicated to serving God and others.

My journey has profoundly illustrated that true wealth is not defined by our material possessions but rather by the unshakeable depth of our faith, the love we choose to share, and the meaningful impact we have on those around us. As I sit down to pen this story, a wave of excitement washes over me. It's a realisation that I have set forth on a transformative journey, one that is far from its conclusion. A fresh chapter of my life is on the horizon, filled with the potential for new experiences and growth.

This new phase will likely present a series of challenges I must navigate, obstacles that will require resilience and a vast world of possibilities that beckons me to explore. Despite any uncertainties that may lie ahead, I hold a steadfast conviction that with God as my guiding light and grace serving as my compass, I will face whatever comes my way with the mindset of a victor, not a victim.

It's a universal truth that life invariably brings its share of storms; a little rain must indeed fall. No one is immune to the trials and tribulations that pop up unexpectedly. However, within those moments of difficulty lies a crucial choice that we must make: will we embrace the role of a victor or succumb to that of a victim?

Choosing to be a victor is not only a better path but profoundly rewarding, especially when we lean on God—the source of all comfort and the keeper of our security. This understanding is at the heart of the message conveyed in this poem, illuminating the strength found in faith and the transformative power of choosing hope and resilience over despair:

> *From the moment we enter this world, we are gifted with the intrinsic right to freedom and fairness. However, none of us can truly anticipate the myriad of experiences that life will present. For some, the path can unfold with smoothness and joy, filled with*

moments of laughter and delight. Yet, for others, the journey can be riddled with uncertainty, presenting numerous obstacles that can seem insurmountable.

Each day may bring with it setbacks that feel overwhelming and beyond our control. In the more difficult phases of life, our struggles can feel more painful than enduring physical torment, akin to being constantly pricked by thorns. Every milestone we reach may feel heavy with complexities and struggles weighing us down.

At times, the very thought of continuing forward can become unbearably heavy, compounded by the fear of whether we will survive the trials we encounter. In these moments, it may appear that there is no escape from our burdens. While some may find themselves cocooned in comfort, with well-made beds awaiting them, others are forced to make do, enduring the harsh realities of life as they lie on 'plantain leaves' through long, dark nights filled with uncertainty and hardship.

Nevertheless, amidst these challenges, it is crucial to cultivate resilience. We possess the power to navigate through life's difficulties, no matter how daunting they may seem. Each of us has a choice: to refuse the role of a victim and instead strive for personal triumph, hoping that dawn will break following the darkness.

It is vital to approach every challenge with the mindset of a victor rather than succumbing to fear. By choosing positivity in the face of adversity, we can transform our struggles into stepping stones for growth. Challenges arise not to dismantle us but to shape our character and strengthen our resolve. Therefore, remain steadfast and strong, for it is through perseverance that we can emerge victorious over life's trials.

A well-known Yoruba proverb states, *"Omi tí èníyàn bá yàn láti mu kò ní ṣàn kọjá ọkan,"* which translates to, "The water that one is destined to drink will never flow past one." This profound saying conveys a significant message: everything one is meant to become or achieve in life will come to fruition. It emphasises the belief in fate and the idea that a higher force guides our paths. With this wisdom in mind, I reflect on the next steps in my journey and realise that I am being gently pushed toward my true calling. I feel a sense of readiness and anticipation as I embark on this new chapter.

CHAPTER 6

The Transformative Journey

Ephesians 2:10 (NIV)

"For we are God's handiwork, created in Christ Jesus to do good works, which God prepared in advance for us to do."

Chapter 6: A Transformative Journey

In the stillness of the night in 1995, a profound whisper echoed within my heart while I was in Reading, United Kingdom. A gentle yet compelling call conveyed, *"Build me an auditorium, and I will cause men to come."* The following morning, as I awoke, a tempest of questions swirled in my mind, igniting a storm of doubt and fear about what this revelation might mean for my life. Yet, beneath that swirling chaos, a spark of hope began to take root. I pondered the possibility that this was meant to be—an earnest calling from God rather than mere whimsy. Initially, I tried to dismiss the notion; my mind raced with rationalisations. I reasoned that perhaps it was just an inexplicable feeling, a fleeting notion tied to a mid-life crisis. I immersed myself in my work to quell the growing unrest within me, hoping to drown out the whispers that echoed persistently in the background.

At that time, I was acutely aware of a significant absence within the community—specifically, a lack of African churches in Reading. This city, bustling with life, was home to numerous African and Black communities yearning for spiritual connection and integration. Some community members found themselves travelling to London every weekend, often at considerable expense, to attend churches that resonated with their cultural identities. Despite the sense of belonging they found at the Africa Christian Fellowship (ACF), UK, there was an unmistakable longing for multicultural churches that embraced their unique expressions of Christianity. The realisation of this profound spiritual need stirred something within me—a long-dormant desire to use my life for a purpose far greater than pursuing a career in Medical Physics.

But first, reflecting on how my Christian journey began is essential. I grew up in Nigeria, immersed in an environment characterised by what I describe as nominal Christianity. Many in my surroundings were religious in name only; they adhered to their church or denomination but did not venture beyond the superficiality of their faith. Their understanding of Christianity seemed limited to attending church services, reading their Bibles sporadically, and offering occasional prayers. Despite doing the outward motions of a "Christian," they were missing out on the profound power, peace, and joy that accompany a genuinely abundant life, as promised in Scripture. This counterfeit version of Christianity eventually became a burden that offered little comfort in the face of life's inevitable storms. I understood that God doesn't call anyone to this lacklustre existence, marked by rituals and traditions; rather, He invites us into a personal relationship characterised by abundance.

My authentic encounter with Jesus occurred during my university years while studying Engineering Physics. One of my Professors would often inscribe on the top corner of the blackboard, *"And God said, let there be light, and there was light,"* before commencing his lectures. This statement perplexed me for quite some time; I struggled to see how such a declaration related to the intricate world of physics. It wasn't until my final year that I mustered the courage to approach him and delve deeper into the significance of those words. In our conversations, he guided me toward understanding the essence of personal relationships with God and the concept of abundant life. This conversation marked the initiation of my genuine Christian walk in 1983. There were no divine flashes or dramatic encounters; instead, a gradual awakening to faith started transforming my life.

Over the years, the seeds of faith began to flourish, allowing me to grow as a committed Christian. I matured in my journey and found various avenues to serve God, participating in house group fellowships, multinational and interdenominational fellowships, and taking on the roles of church elder and member of the Board of Trustees. These experiences outside my professional life were made possible by God's grace, driving home the idea that my life could serve a purpose larger than myself. It was a journey that had transformed me from a seeker into a servant, filled with a renewed sense of calling.

In the calm stillness of 1995, I sensed a celestial whisper, a profound calling that echoed deep within my soul. It grew ever more intense, urging me to take action. Feeling the weight of uncertainty, I sought guidance, clarity, and the wisdom to navigate the path ahead. I turned to my wife and two dear Christian family friends, whose lives overflowed with compassion and insight. Their unwavering spiritual counsel had always been a beacon for us.

Deeply attuned to the subtleties of spiritual insights, these friends listened with genuine interest. They offered words of encouragement, each phrase steeped in love and understanding. They emphasised the essential nature of prayer and discernment, highlighting the importance of seeking God's will through His Word and the sensible advice of those who had traversed similar paths before me. One particular friend urged me to take time for reflection, insisting, "Seek God's will through prayer and Scripture. Do not hesitate to ask for wisdom and guidance; He will not abandon you on this journey."

Pastor Michael Adeyemi, who has since passed, perceived that my calling extended beyond merely constructing a physical church building. He recognised it as a potential endeavour to establish a network of believers, a community bound together in faith. At that moment, the embryonic concept of a network began to take shape in my mind. Yet, as I searched for a physical auditorium to fulfil this vision, life's currents unexpectedly swept me away to another city, causing the vision to fade from my immediate focus.

Chapter 6: A Transformative Journey

As the years unfolded, a significant moment arrived during a sacred prayer time in 2007. It was then that the once-dormant vision resurfaced with renewed vigour. My heart began to pivot toward primary missionary work, igniting a passion I had previously set aside. The initial mission to South Africa materialised, undertaken with a diverse team of committed Christian professionals, each dedicated to covering their costs. Their collective effort bore fruit, manifesting in community empowerment and a mobile medical ministry that ventured into a remote district, largely untouched by modernity. We converted a trailer into a makeshift dispensary, providing essential healthcare and sowing seeds of hope grounded in the Gospel. The mission's far-reaching impact extended beyond medical care; it embraced the neglected rural populace through tangible support, education, and spiritual nourishment during a dire need.

The enthusiasm for missionary work blossomed further, leading to Uganda in 2019. Through the support of the ACF, we endeavoured to uplift disadvantaged children, focusing on their education, healthcare, and basic sustenance. We were planting seeds of change across East Africa. The whisper that had once been a gentle sound in my mind became a constant companion, a persistent nudge prompting me to confront the questions that I had long avoided.

As time unfolded, a profound concern began to gnaw at my soul. I felt a keen unease as I observed the sacred platforms bestowed by God being misused to lead His people astray. Many pastors and ministers of the Gospel were, perhaps unknowingly, directing their congregants away from their unique professional callings, thereby contributing to wider societal challenges. This growing concern birthed a calling within me akin to that of a marketplace Apostle, an ambassador of Christ whose mission was to leverage divine investments and blessings to illuminate the world with the unadulterated truth of His Word.

In response to this divine imperative, RadiantLink Ministries emerged in 2024. Fueled by an unwavering passion to dispel darkness with the radiant light of God's teachings, I embarked on a transformative journey alongside a fellow minister, Pastor Oluwatimilehin Ologunoye, into the realm of digital ministry. We aspired to utilise technology and media platforms as tools to spread our message. This ministry is a testament to an earnest commitment to counterbalance the dilution of God's Word, providing an unwavering source of enlightenment in a world that desperately seeks divine truth and clarity.

RadiantLink Ministries emerged as a luminous beacon of hope, dedicated to spreading the undiluted Word of God throughout the expansive digital landscape. Its mission

Chapter 6: A Transformative Journey

is to touch hearts, dispel the shadows of uncertainty, and enlighten souls on their spiritual journeys. The moment I decided to establish this ministry, I felt as if the entire world around me transformed. This shift unleashed a wave of exhilaration and a realm of new opportunities that lay before me. I understood that this choice would irrevocably alter the course of my life, propelling me into a deeper purpose that I had long sought.

Since its inception, RadiantLink Ministries has made a phenomenal impact across diverse communities around the globe. Through initiatives like the Daily Devotional, individuals are provided with daily inspiration, encouraging them to reflect on their spiritual lives. The Podcast, which delves into contemporary topics pertinent to our times, has fostered engaging discussions that resonate with listeners, inviting them to dialogue about faith in the modern world. Meanwhile, the Monthly Global Prayer Meeting serves as a powerful uniting force, connecting individuals across continents and creating a tapestry of prayer transcending geographical boundaries. Additionally, the TV documentaries produced through the ministry provide compelling narratives that explore faith, resilience, and the human experience. We also regularly share inspirational content across social media platforms, amplifying our reach and uplifting countless souls. Witnessing the significant development and growth of RadiantLink Ministries fills my heart with gratitude and joy.

In those pivotal moments of reflection, I heard an almost ethereal whisper within me, affirming, "This is it; this is where you are meant to be." The transition from a life focused on personal ambition and professional accomplishments to one devoted to service and faith marked a profound turning point in my existence. During this introspective journey, I began to grasp the deeper calling that had been gently echoing in the silence of my heart. I pondered why God had preserved me through years of unexpected trials and tribulations. I understood that God's unique plan remains steadfast, independent of the unpredictable circumstances that life presents. Our situations do not dictate our destiny; it is God who guides our steps. Despite the inevitable bumps, turns, detours, hills, and valleys life may bring, I believe that His enduring grace is always present, sustaining and uplifting me.

Embracing ministry has been nothing short of a transformative journey, akin to shedding an old skin in favour of a renewed identity. I left behind the structured familiarity of a professional career to step into the liberating realm of faith and service. While the path ahead is undoubtedly lined with its own challenges and triumphs, each milestone will deepen my understanding and enrich my journey, weaving a rich tapestry of experiences that shape who I am becoming.

CHAPTER 7

The God Factor

John 1:12 (NIV)

"Yet to all who did receive him, to those who believed in his name, he gave the right to become children of God."

Chapter 7: The God Factor

Throughout my life, I have vividly shared various episodes from my journey, hoping to inspire you to embark on your own adventure and create unforgettable memories that will last a lifetime. Each experience serves as a powerful reflection, allowing for an introspective journey that, when articulated, offers a unique perspective that can bless the world. It is not merely about recalling past events—it's about capturing the essence of personal growth, the lessons learned along the way, and the meaningful impact we can have on the lives of others. My deepest desire is to ensure that others can glean insights from everything I have discovered about myself throughout this journey.

"Is this the end of the journey?" you might wonder. The answer is likely, "No!" The conclusion of one chapter often marks the beginning of another. It represents a significant transition—from what has been familiar to the excitement of the unknown. Each ending is not merely a closure but a doorway to new possibilities and experiences waiting to unfold. This cycle of endings and beginnings is a beautiful reminder that life is, in many ways, a mosaic of interconnected journeys. Each path carries its own distinct narrative and destination, underscoring that one journey inevitably leads to another, creating a continuum of experiences. This ongoing cycle reflects the grace of God bestowed upon all His creation.

Reflecting on my own life, I often ponder an intriguing question: *If my biological father had been a more active presence from the very beginning, would my life have played out differently? Would I have become more, less, or equally successful?* This pervasive query has lingered in my mind countless times. It leads me to explore the profound concept of what I refer to as "The God Factor" that resides within each of us. Through introspection, I have realised that grace is not merely a reward dispensed based on good or bad actions, nor is it an accolade to be earned. Rather, it is an extraordinary gift—freely given and wrapped in unconditional love. This grace has been my steadfast companion, guiding me from conception, shielding me from myriad potential catastrophes, and presenting me with countless opportunities that have shaped who I am today. It is this same grace that every person needs in their life, for no human being or external force can redefine what grace has already destined for us. I firmly think that there was a special reason and intention behind my birth.

> *"For I know the plans I have for you," declares the LORD. "They are plans for good and not for disaster, to give you a future and a hope" - Jeremiah 29:11 (NLV).*

Grace can lead us toward good plans, a promising future, and a sense of hope. The notion of "The God

Factor" is utilised in various contexts to acknowledge a divine superior influence in all areas of our lives, asserting that only God can achieve what may seem impossible. This term also finds its place in literature; for example, Cathleen Falsani's illuminating book, "The God Factor: Inside the Spiritual Lives of Public People," explores the spiritual journeys of influential figures and how their belief systems shape their actions and the societal landscape. The core message is profound: the quality of who we are is determined not by external influences but by what God instils within us. The God Factor manifests as a reflection of divine nature and character, as a vessel for His love in action, and as a foundation for our walk of faith.

While our upbringing and environment can impact us, they do not dictate our ultimate identity. What truly matters is the conscious choice of who we become and how we choose to navigate our lives. More certainly, our identity hinges on how we embrace and utilise the God Factor within us. This divine influence empowers us to forge our path and define our legacy.

The Bible's compelling story of Joseph is woven through a complex web of family dynamics, interpersonal relationships, and personal growth. Born into a complex and polygamous family, Joseph was the eleventh son of Jacob, favoured above his eleven brothers, which set the stage for his blessings and trials. Joseph was a dreamer

Against All Odds

as a child, receiving prophetic visions that he eagerly shared with his brothers. However, these revelations sparked jealousy and resentment in their hearts, leading to tragic events.

Joseph's life took a dramatic turn when his brothers, driven by envy, plotted against him. They cast him into a pit and ultimately sold him into slavery in Egypt, stripping him of his comfortable upbringing. This unjust treatment was merely the beginning of a long journey characterised by adversity. As an enslaved person, Joseph experienced betrayal and false accusations, culminating in his imprisonment. Interestingly, even in the darkest times, Joseph never lost sight of his dreams or faith.

In prison, Joseph's remarkable ability to interpret dreams came to the forefront, catching the attention of Pharaoh. When presented with the chance to interpret Pharaoh's troubling dreams, Joseph demonstrated his gift and his unwavering faith in God's plan. His interpretations foresaw seven years of abundance followed by seven years of famine. This prophetic insight led to his rise from prisoner to the second most powerful figure in Egypt, where he was tasked with saving the nation from impending disaster.

Joseph's later reflections reveal a profound understanding of divine intervention. In Genesis 50:19-21

(ERV), when confronted by his brothers, he expressed forgiveness and compassion, asserting:

> "Don't be afraid. I am not God! I have no right to punish you. It is true that you planned to do something bad to me. But really, God was planning good things. God's plan was to use me to save the lives of many people. And that is what happened. So don't be afraid. I will take care of you and your children."

His acknowledgement of "The God Factor" reveals that despite human intentions, divine purpose prevails. Joseph's story illustrates that life's challenges, rather than defining our destinies, can propel us toward greatness when aligned with a higher purpose.

The concept of "The God Factor" extends beyond Joseph's narrative, offering a powerful reminder of hope and potential in our own lives. The Scripture declares in Lamentations 3:22, *"It is of the Lord's mercies that we are not consumed because his compassions fail not."* It emphasises that our circumstances do not bind us; our intrinsic worth and potential come from being created in God's image, as stated in Genesis 1:26 and 28. God's empowering love embraces our endeavours, encouraging us to be fruitful and multiply.

We all possess an innate influence capable of yielding extraordinary outcomes. The possibilities are boundless when God is at the centre of our lives. The "God Factor" encapsulates the wonders of divine attributes—faith, love, favour, mercy, wisdom, creativity, forgiveness, kindness, and joy—being abundant within us. These attributes and our inner strength and resilience act as trump cards that pave the way for boundless greatness and success.

As I reflect upon this narrative, my heart swells with gratitude and praise to the Almighty God, who sustains me through the trials and triumphs of life. Unlike the transient and hollow deities that permeate the world, the Lord is eternal and infinite, unmatched in all perfections. He has embraced the role of my protector, provider, and saviour through every challenge I face against seemingly insurmountable odds. His essence—purity, holiness, goodness, wisdom, and power—shines through each glorious act of creation and grace He has bestowed upon me. For this, I remain thankful for the incredible blessings, both temporal and spiritual, that the Lord continually enriches my life with. Truly, the Lord God is uniquely and wondrously sovereign!

CHAPTER 8

Rise Above Prejudice and Discrimination

Romans 2:11 (AMPC)

"For God shows no partiality [undue favour or unfairness; with Him one man is not different from another]."

Chapter 8: Rise Above Prejudice/Discrimination

I wanted this book to be more than just a simple memoir; my goal was to write something that tells a higher spiritual story while sharing personal experiences and important life lessons that anyone can relate to. With this in mind, I decided to place this section at the end of the book. I believe that my story wouldn't be complete or meaningful without discussing the important issues of injustice and prejudice I've experienced.

Prejudice means having unfair opinions about people or groups without really understanding their stories or experiences. This issue is widespread and affects both individuals and society in serious ways, often leading to outcomes that can change lives. Prejudice is deeply rooted in society, showing up in institutions, communities, and personal relationships. It creates a tangled mess of assumptions that go unchecked.

Prejudice can show itself in many ways, from subtle unfairness at work to outright hostility in daily life. It can shape how people think and act, leading to a skewed view of the world that keeps misunderstandings alive. As a result, prejudice creates divisions within society, building walls between different groups and making it difficult for people to communicate and understand one another. This division weakens the bonds that hold us together and prevents us from working together to find solutions and create communities where everyone can succeed.

Based on my own experiences and observations in various situations—ranging from everyday conversations to larger social movements—I want to share my thoughts and contribute to strategies that can help counteract negative biases and promote understanding and unity instead of division.

One significant experience stood out in 1991. I approached my PhD supervisor for a job reference, and he refused to write one, saying, *"Though you are a brilliant student, working in the UK isn't for you because of your* **strong accent**.*"*

In 2014, I went to a Land Rover dealership looking to buy a new Range Rover Sport. The salesperson said discourteously to me, *"We don't discount our vehicles because we sell to* **high-class people**.*"*

Another day, while I was washing my Range Rover Sport outside my home, a man walking his dog approached me and asked, *"Don't you think this car is* **too big for you**?*"*

These incidents are just a few examples of prejudice I've encountered, and while it's hard to remember them all, I want to share one in more detail because of its lasting impact on me.

Chapter 8: Rise Above Prejudice/Discrimination

This story begins at the start of my career with the National Health Service (NHS). After completing my PhD in Medical Physics, which required years of hard work, I took on a job at a particular hospital. This new role opened the door to a fresh chapter in my professional life, filled with both opportunities and challenges. I was the only Black African and the only person with a doctorate in a team of thirty people dedicated to supporting cancer treatment.

As part of my onboarding process, I participated in a program designed to help new employees understand their roles and how they could grow within the department. Within our team, there was one senior staff member who was responsible for overseeing work schedules and assigning projects. Unfortunately, this person was unhappy with my appointment because he had not taken part in the interview and recruitment process. His displeasure soon turned into open hostility. I became the target of negative comments that resonated throughout the department, and he unfairly questioned my skills in front of coworkers.

It didn't take long for the conflict between us to become obvious, leading to a series of unfair actions over time. He started giving me less important tasks and took away opportunities that could have helped me grow in my career. My assignments often felt unbalanced, making it hard to work together with him. It seemed like he wanted me to fail, possibly hoping I would make mistakes that could hurt my career. Some of my coworkers even noticed the workplace was becoming more hostile because of this ongoing tension.

At first, I was overwhelmed with disappointment and frustration. Sharing an office with him only added to my stress. I had always believed in treating everyone with respect and equality, so I was unprepared for such obvious hostility. Unsure of how to deal with the situation, I talked to my wife and a trusted colleague. They encouraged me to express my feelings to the head of the department.

Even though I wanted to report him right away, I decided to first approach him informally to share my concerns. To my surprise, he brushed off what I had to say, and nothing changed. Eventually, I brought my concerns to the head of the department, who promised to address the issue. He insisted that our workplace didn't tolerate prejudice or discrimination. However, not long after, I learned that the staff member had denied my claims, and I was told to drop the matter. Sadly, the negative behaviour continued, but it became more hidden.

There was a moment when I seriously thought about changing jobs to escape the situation, but my wife advised against it. She pointed out that I might face similar problems in a new job and suggested we continue seeking guidance. She encouraged me to find support and consider filing a formal complaint if things became too difficult to handle.

Amid all these challenges, an unexpected opportunity came that changed everything. With the backing of the head of the department, I proposed a new process that would improve our patient care. To my surprise, the proposal was well-received and even earned professional recognition, leading to an award and marking our department's first publication. This success marked a big turning point, and soon after, the negative treatment I had faced began to fade away completely.

In the end, the staff member who once treated me badly came forward to admit his past negative feelings, expressed deep regret for his behaviour, and offered a sincere apology. This raises the question: *Are there ways to combat prejudice and discrimination at work?* Absolutely! As this story shows, several key elements can help, such as consistently performing well at work, staying persistent until things improve, holding onto your values, being ready to forgive, and keeping the possibility of friendship alive. These concepts were my guiding light through this experience. Amid all the prejudice, I climbed up the career ladder to become the head of the same department.

Prejudice is not just a simple issue; it's a serious moral problem that runs deep within us and reflects bigger issues in society. This idea is echoed in the Bible, specifically in the book of Luke 6:45, which says that *"a good person brings good things out of their heart, while a bad person brings bad things."* Just like a healthy tree produces good fruit, a caring heart only produces good actions. We can tell a lot about someone based on how they speak.

If someone frequently shows anger, rudeness, or immorality, it's a good indication of their true character. On the flip side, if someone is kind, supportive, and polite all the time, that's likely who they are on the inside. While some people may pretend to be something they're not; eventually, their true character will show through. What we say reflects what is really in our hearts.

In closing, I request the reader's indulgence as I share my journey, which has been filled with diverse experiences and valuable lessons. Each moment is like a small snapshot of my life—brief but significant. If any part seems unengaging, I hope you can appreciate that every experience has shaped who I am and influenced my decisions. I believe that both our personal experiences and the things happening around us play a huge role in shaping our future. Everything we go through, the choices we make, and the paths we take all contribute to what comes next, making our journey toward the future more exciting. It's essential to look ahead with curiosity, stay positive, and be open to learning and growing. Even though we can't predict everything that will happen, we can choose how to respond to whatever life sends our way.

Glossary

The word "Iya" translates to "Mother" in Yoruba, reflecting the culture's deep respect and affection associated with motherhood.

The term "Baba" means "Father" in Yoruba, signifying fathers' important role as protectors and providers within the family unit.

'Ikere-Ekiti' is a notable city in Nigeria's Ekiti State, renowned for its rich history and cultural heritage. It serves as one of the significant urban centres in the region.

"Ado-Ekiti," the capital city of Ekiti State, derives its name from the Yoruba term "Ado." This bustling city is a hub of governance and commerce within the state, characterised by a vibrant community and numerous cultural landmarks.

"Irona" is a specific community located within Ado-Ekiti. It is known for its unique local culture and traditions, contributing to the diverse tapestry of the city.

The term "Oga" refers to an individual who wields power, influence, or status within a community or organisation.

It generally denotes someone with a senior position, such as a boss or leader.

"Lagos," often called Lagos City, is a sprawling metropolitan area in southwestern Nigeria. It is recognised as the country's economic capital and principal port, famous for its dynamic economy and diverse population.

In the Yoruba language, "Ode" means "hunter." This term reflects the significance of hunting in certain cultural practices and its role in the community.

The phrase "Omo Baba" translates to "father's son" in Yoruba, signifying a direct lineage and familial connection to one's father, emphasising the importance of paternal relationships within the culture.

SUPPORTING RESOURCES

The hyperlinks below direct you to the supplementary resources referenced in this book.

RadiantLink Ministries link:
linktr.ee/radiantlinkministries

https://www.fatherhood.org/father-absence-statistic

By visiting these resources, learn about the benefits of father involvement and how to become a father-inclusive organisation.

NOTES

NOTES

www.ingramcontent.com/pod-product-compliance
Lightning Source LLC
Chambersburg PA
CBHW041146110526
44590CB00027B/4137